THE CONSULTANT'S PATH:

A FREELANCER'S GUIDE TO
ACHIEVING SUCCESS

IMA .J. BROWN

COPYRIGHT

TABLE OF CONTENTS

Introduction

In the realm of modern work, where flexibility, independence, and the pursuit of passion have become paramount, the freelance consultant stands as a shining example of what's possible. They are the architects of their own careers, the masters of their crafts, and the entrepreneurs of their destinies. If you're holding this book in your hands or reading these words on your screen, it's because you are one of them—a freelance consultant with dreams and aspirations.

Welcome to "The Consultant's Path: A Freelancer's Guide to Achieving Success." Within these pages, you'll embark on a journey of self-discovery, skill mastery, and business acumen—a journey that will equip you with the knowledge and tools you need to not just survive but thrive in the dynamic world of freelance consulting.

In the following chapters, we will delve deep into the intricacies of the consulting profession. We'll explore how to find your niche, create an irresistible personal brand, and attract clients who value your expertise. We'll uncover the secrets of effective project management and time optimization, ensuring that you not only meet your clients' expectations but exceed them.

The financial aspects of freelancing are often a stumbling block for many. Fear not; we will guide you through pricing strategies, budgeting techniques, and financial management principles that will put you in control of your earnings. Additionally, you'll learn about the legal considerations and contracts that protect your interests and those of your clients.

Success as a freelance consultant isn't just about the technical skills you possess—it's also about the relationships you build. We will delve into the art of nurturing client relations, from the initial contact to long-term partnerships. And when challenges arise, as they inevitably will, you'll be equipped with strategies for resolving conflicts and maintaining your professional integrity.

The path to success is paved through continuous learning. In this book, we'll explore avenues for professional growth, from courses and workshops to self-study and mentorship. Staying relevant in your field and adapting to changing industry landscapes will become second nature.

But success isn't solely defined by your career; it's also about achieving a fulfilling work-life balance. You'll find guidance on setting boundaries, avoiding burnout, and ensuring that your consulting journey aligns with your broader life goals.

"The Consultant's Path" isn't just about theory; it's about action.
In the ever-evolving world of consulting, staying ahead of the curve is essential. We'll explore emerging trends and opportunities in the field, enabling you to position yourself as a trailblazer, ready to seize new avenues for growth and innovation.Each chapter of this book is a stepping stone on your journey to success, and I encourage you to actively engage with the content.

By the end of "The Consultant's Path," my hope is that you will not only be equipped with the tools and strategies needed for success but also inspired to craft a career that's uniquely your own—a career that's a reflection of your skills, passions, and aspirations.

Your dreams are within reach, and this book is your guide. It's time to embark on "The Consultant's Path" and make your mark as a thriving freelance consultant.

With excitement for your journey ahead,

[IMA J BROWN]
Author of "The Consultant's Path: A Freelancer's Guide

CHAPTER 1

Starting Your Consulting Journey

Defining Your Consulting Niche and Specialization: A Blueprint for Freelance Success

As you step into the world of freelance consulting, one of the most pivotal decisions you'll make is defining your niche and specialization. Think of this choice as the cornerstone of your consulting business. It's not just about what you offer; it's about what makes you unique in a crowded marketplace.

Why is defining your niche so crucial?
Imagine you're in a large library, and you want to find a specific book. You'd head to the section that matches your topic of interest, right? In the same way, when potential clients seek consulting services, they're searching for experts who specialize in solving their particular problems. This is where your niche comes into play.

Here are some guiding principles to help you pinpoint your consulting niche and specialization:

1. Reflect on Your Passion and Expertise:

Before diving into the market, take a moment to reflect on what you're truly passionate about and where your expertise lies. What particular topics or niche excite you? What knowledge and skills do you possess that set you apart from the competition? Your niche should align with your passions and strengths, as this will not only make your work more enjoyable but also inspire confidence in potential clients.

2. Identify Market Needs:

Research is your best friend when identifying your niche. Study the market and identify areas where there is demand for your services. Look for gaps in the market where your unique skills can provide solutions. Talk to potential clients, industry experts, and peers to gain insights into what problems need solving.

3. Consider Your Target Audience:

Your niche should also align with your target audience. Who are the clients you want to serve? What are their difficulties and challenges? Tailor your specialization to meet the needs of your ideal clients. This alignment will make your marketing efforts more effective.

4. Start Narrow, Expand Later:

It's often wise to start with a relatively narrow niche and expand your services as you gain experience and a client base. This allows you to establish yourself as an expert in a specific area before diversifying. Over time, you can broaden your specialization if you desire.

5. Test and Iterate:

Don't be afraid to test your niche and make adjustments as needed. Your initial choice may evolve as you gain experience and insights into what works best for you and your clients. Be flexible and open to change.

6. Craft Your Unique Value Proposition:

Once you've defined your niche, craft a compelling value proposition. Clearly communicate what makes you the go-to expert in your chosen area. Explain how your specialized knowledge and skills benefit clients and help them achieve their goals.

7. Stay Informed and Evolve:

The consulting landscape is ever-changing. Stay informed about industry trends, emerging technologies, and evolving client needs within your niche. Adapt and evolve your skills and services accordingly to remain a valuable resource.

Defining your consulting niche and specialization is not a one-time task but an ongoing process of refinement. Embrace the journey, be open to learning, and remember that your niche should not limit your potential but amplify your expertise. As you align your passions with market needs, you're well on your way to becoming a sought-after freelance consultant in your chosen domain.

Setting Up Your Freelance Consulting Business: A Financial and Legal Guide for New Consultants

Congratulations on taking the leap into the world of freelance consulting! Starting your own consulting business is an exciting venture, but it also requires careful financial and legal planning to ensure your venture's success and compliance with regulations.

Here's a comprehensive guide to help you get started on the right financial and legal footing:

1. Business Structure:

Choose a Legal Structure: Decide whether you want to operate as a sole proprietor, form an LLC, or establish another business structure. Each has its own implications for taxes, liability, and reporting.

2. Business Name and Registration:

- Choose a Unique Business Name: Select a name that reflects your consulting services and is not already in use by another business in your area.

- Register Your Business: Depending on your location, you may need to register your business name with the appropriate government agency. This is usually done at the state or local level.

3. Tax Identification Number:

Obtain an EIN: An Employer Identification Number (EIN) is required for tax purposes. You can apply for an EIN through the IRS website.

4. Business Licenses and Permits:

Check Local Requirements: Research and obtain any necessary licenses or permits to legally operate your consulting business in your area. This may include zoning permits or professional licenses.

5. Business Insurance:

Consider Liability Insurance: Depending on your consulting services, it may be wise to invest in professional liability insurance to protect yourself from potential legal claims.

6. Business Banking:

Open a Separate Business Account: Keep your personal and business finances separate by opening a dedicated business bank account. This simplifies accounting and tax reporting.

7. Accounting and Record-Keeping:

- **Set Up an Accounting System:** Implement an accounting system to track income and expenses. Consider using accounting software or hiring an accountant.

- **Keep Records:** Maintain accurate records of all financial transactions, including invoices, receipts, and bank statements.

8. Pricing and Invoicing:

- Determine Your Pricing Strategy: Decide how you will price your consulting services. Consider hourly rates, project-based fees, or retainer agreements.

- Create Professional Invoices: Develop a standard invoice template with all necessary details, including payment terms and contact information.

9. Taxes:

- Understand Tax Obligations: Familiarize yourself with tax regulations for self-employed individuals in your jurisdiction.

- Set Aside Taxes: Save a portion of your earnings for quarterly estimated taxes to avoid a large tax bill at the end of the year.

10. Contracts:

Create Clear Contracts: Draft comprehensive contracts for your consulting projects. Clearly outline project scope, deliverables, payment terms, deadlines, and dispute resolution procedures.

11. Client Agreements:

Establish Client Agreements: Ensure your clients sign written agreements that detail the services you'll provide, fees, timelines, and any other pertinent terms.

12. Intellectual Property:

Address Ownership: Clearly state in your contracts who owns intellectual property rights to work produced during consulting engagements.

13. Data Protection and Privacy:

Comply with Data Privacy Laws: If you handle client data, be aware of and comply with data protection regulations, such as GDPR or CCPA, depending on your client base.

14. Professional Advice:

Consult Professionals: When in doubt about legal or financial matters, seek advice from legal and financial professionals who specialize in small businesses or freelancers.

Starting a freelance consulting business is a rewarding endeavor, but it's essential to set up a solid financial and legal foundation. Doing so not only ensures your compliance with regulations but also helps you establish trust and credibility with clients. With careful planning and attention to these details, you're on your way to building a successful consulting career.

Building a Strong Online Presence and Personal Brand for New Freelance Consultants

In today's digital age, establishing a professional online presence and crafting a compelling personal brand is essential for freelance consultants. Your online presence serves as your virtual storefront, and your personal brand is what sets you apart from the competition. Here's a step-by-step guide to help you build a robust online presence and develop a memorable personal brand as a new freelance consultant:

1. Define Your Brand Identity:
   - **Start with Self-Reflection:** Identify your unique strengths, values, and passions. What makes you stand out in your field? What niche or brand do you want to be known for?
   - **Determine Your Target Audience:** Understand your ideal clients, their needs, and their pain points. Tailor your brand to resonate with them.

2. Craft a Clear Brand Message:

- **Develop a Value Proposition:** Summarize what you offer and why it matters to your clients. This should be concise and impactful.

- **Create a Tagline:** A memorable tagline can encapsulate your brand message and make you more memorable.

3. Build a Professional Website:

- **Register a Domain Name:** Choose a domain name that reflects your brand and is easy to remember.

- **Create a User-Friendly Website:** Design a clean, easy-to-navigate website that showcases your services, portfolio, testimonials, and contact information.

- **Use High-Quality Content:** Populate your website with informative blog posts, case studies, and other valuable content related to your niche.

4. Optimize for Search Engines (SEO):

- **Research Keywords:** Identify relevant keywords for your industry and incorporate them naturally into your website content.

- **Optimize Meta Tags:** Craft compelling meta titles and descriptions for each page to improve search engine visibility.

5. Leverage Social Media:

- **Choose the Right Platforms:** Determine which social media platforms your target audience frequents and focus your efforts there.

- **Maintain Consistency:** Use the same profile picture, bio, and messaging across all social media profiles.

- **Share Valuable Content:** Regularly share industry insights, tips, and your own expertise to establish yourself as a thought leader.

6. Create a LinkedIn Profile:

- **Optimize Your Profile:** Complete your LinkedIn profile with a professional photo, detailed work experience, and compelling summary.

- **Network Actively:** Connect with industry professionals, engage in relevant groups, and share your knowledge through articles and posts.

7. Guest Blogging and Content Contribution:

- **Offer to Write Guest Posts:** Reach out to reputable industry blogs and offer to contribute guest articles.

- Publish on LinkedIn or Medium: Use these platforms to share your expertise and gain visibility among a broader audience.

8. Online Portfolio:

- Showcase Your Work: Create an online portfolio that highlights your successful projects, case studies, and client testimonials.

- Keep It Updated: Regularly update your portfolio to reflect your latest work and achievements.

9. Engage with Your Audience:

- Respond to Comments: Engage with your audience by responding to comments and messages promptly.

- Host Webinars or Workshops: Offer webinars or online workshops to share your knowledge and connect with potential clients.

10. Collect and Display Testimonials:

- Request Feedback: Ask satisfied clients for testimonials and showcase them prominently on your website and social media profiles.

11. Networking and Outreach:

- **Attend Virtual Events:** Participate in webinars, conferences, and virtual networking events within your industry.

- **Connect Personally:** Reach out to potential clients or collaborators with personalized messages expressing your interest in their work.

12. Measure Your Progress:

- **Use Analytics:** Monitor website traffic, social media engagement, and the effectiveness of your branding efforts. Adjust your strategy as needed.

Building a professional online presence and personal brand is an ongoing process. It takes time to establish yourself and gain recognition in your field. Stay consistent, adapt to industry changes, and always provide value to your audience. Over time, your brand will become a powerful asset in attracting clients and advancing your freelance consulting career.

CHAPTER 2

Client Acquisition and Marketing

As a newbie freelance consultant, finding and attracting clients can be a challenging yet essential aspect of building your consulting business. Here are some effective strategies to help you get started:

1. Identify Your Ideal Client:

Begin by defining your ideal client. Consider factors such as industry, company size, location, and specific challenges they face. This will help you target your efforts more effectively.

2. Local Networking:

Attend local business networking events, meet ups and chamber of commerce meetings. Face to face networking can be especially effective for building trust and rapport.

3. Online Presence:

Build a professional website that showcases your services, expertise, and portfolio. Optimize it for search engines (SEO) to increase your visibility in online searches. Consider starting a blog or sharing valuable content related to your niche to establish yourself as an expert.

4. LinkedIn:

Create a compelling LinkedIn profile that highlights your skills and experience as a consultant. Connect with relevant professionals and engage in industry groups. Share your insights and participate in discussions to boost your visibility.

5. Social Media:

Use social media platforms like Twitter, Facebook, or Instagram to share your knowledge and engage with your target audience. Share valuable content. Social media advertising can also be effective for reaching a broader audience.

6. Freelance Platforms:

Join freelance platforms like Upwork, Freelancer, or Fiverr to find clients looking for consulting services. These platforms can help you build your portfolio and gain initial experience.

7. Networking Events:

Attend industry-specific events, conferences, webinars, and workshops. These events provide opportunities to network with potential clients and establish credibility within your field.

8. Cold Outreach:

Reach out to potential clients directly via email or social media. Craft personalized and compelling messages that explain how your consulting services can solve their specific problems. Be prepared for rejection but keep refining your approach.

9. Content Marketing:

Create informative and valuable content such as ebooks, whitepapers, or webinars related to your niche. Offer these resources for free in exchange for email subscriptions, allowing you to build a list of potential clients.

10. Collaborate:

Partner with other consultants, agencies, or professionals in complementary fields. Collaborative projects can expand your reach and introduce you to new clients.

11. Online Marketplaces:

Consider listing your services on specialized online marketplaces for consultants, where clients actively search for expertise in various fields.

12. Client Testimonials:
Encourage satisfied clients to provide testimonials and reviews that you can feature on your website and marketing materials. Positive feedback builds trust with potential clients.

13. Offer Free Workshops or Consultations:
Provide free workshops, webinars, or initial consultations to showcase your expertise. This can be an excellent way to demonstrate your value and convert prospects into paying clients.

14. Paid Advertising:
Invest in targeted online advertising campaigns, such as Google Ads or Facebook Ads, to reach potential clients actively searching for consulting services.

15. Professional Associations:
Join industry-specific professional associations and leverage their networks and resources for client acquisition.

Remember that building a client base takes time, and persistence is key. Be prepared to adapt your strategies based on what works best for your niche and target audience. Continuously refine your approach and focus on delivering exceptional service to your clients, as satisfied clients can become your most significant source of referrals.

Unlocking Success: Digital Marketing and Social Media Tactics for Freelance Consultants

In the modern business landscape, the role of a freelance consultant has evolved from a niche profession to a dynamic and sought-after career choice. The rise of digital technology has empowered individuals to offer their expertise to clients worldwide, transcending geographical boundaries. Yet, the path to success in the realm of freelance consulting is far from simple. To stand out and thrive, consultants must harness the power of digital marketing and social media tactics. In this essay, we'll explore the essential strategies that freelance consultants should master to propel their careers to new heights.

The Digital Transformation of Freelance Consulting

The freelance consulting sector has undergone a profound transformation in recent years, largely driven by digitization. While traditional forms of networking and word-of-mouth referrals still play a crucial role, the digital realm has become an indispensable arena for consultants to showcase their expertise and connect with potential clients. Let's delve into the core digital marketing and social media tactics that are essential for freelance consultants to know and employ:

1. Building a Professional Website:

A consultant's website serves as the virtual headquarters of their business. It's the first place potential clients visit to learn about the consultant's services, expertise, and track record. A well-designed, user-friendly website instills trust and provides a professional image.

2. Search Engine Optimization (SEO):

Understanding the fundamentals of SEO is paramount. Consultants need to optimize their websites for search engines to enhance visibility.

This involves keyword research, meta tag optimization, and the creation of high-quality, SEO-friendly content.

3. Content Marketing Strategy:

Content is the currency of the digital world. Crafting a content marketing strategy that includes blog posts, articles, case studies, or videos helps consultants demonstrate their industry knowledge and establish themselves as thought leaders. Regularly publishing valuable content keeps them engaged with their target audience.

4. Email Marketing Campaigns:

Building an email list of interested prospects is a treasure trove for freelance consultants. By offering valuable resources like ebooks, guides, or newsletters in exchange for email subscriptions, consultants can nurture leads, share insights, and promote their services.

5. Leveraging Social Media:

In the era of social connectivity, having a presence on the right social media platforms is a must. For many consultants, LinkedIn, with its professional networking focus, is a valuable asset. However, consultants should also explore platforms like Twitter, Facebook, or Instagram depending on their niche and target audience.

6. LinkedIn Strategy:

LinkedIn stands out as the primary platform for professional networking. A well-optimized LinkedIn profile featuring a professional photo, detailed work history, and a compelling summary is akin to a digital resume. Engaging with industry peers and participating in relevant groups enhances visibility and networking opportunities.

7. Creating a Social Media Content Calendar:

Consistency is key in social media. Consultants should develop a content calendar to plan and schedule their posts. This ensures a steady stream of content that reinforces their brand identity.

8. Engagement and Interaction:

Social media is not a one-way street. Active participation is vital. Consultants should respond promptly to comments, messages, and interactions on their posts. Engaging with the audience fosters trust and strengthens relationships.

9. Paid Advertising Campaigns:

To reach a broader audience, paid advertising campaigns on platforms like Google Ads or Facebook Ads can be effective. Starting with a modest budget and conducting A/B testing of different ad formats helps identify what resonates best with the audience.

10. Video Marketing:

Video content is a powerful medium to connect with the audience on a personal level. Consultants can use videos for informative content, webinars, or vlogs to showcase their expertise and build a more personal connection.

11. Analytics and Data Analysis:

Digital marketing should be data-driven. Social media analytics and website tracking tools provide insights into performance. By analyzing data, consultants can make informed adjustments to their strategy for better results.

12. Guest Blogging and Collaborations:

Collaborating with industry influencers and guest blogging on relevant websites extends a consultant's reach. These activities position them as experts and provide access to a broader audience.

13. Testimonials and Case Studies:

Client testimonials and case studies are potent tools for building credibility. Highlighting successful outcomes and satisfied clients demonstrates the value a consultant provides. These assets should be prominently featured on the consultant's website and social media profiles.

14. A/B Testing:

The digital realm allows for experimentation. Conducting A/B tests on different headlines, content formats, and calls to action (CTAs) helps consultants refine their marketing materials and maximize their impact.

15. Networking on Social Media:

Social media is not just about content sharing; it's also a platform for networking. Joining relevant LinkedIn groups, participating in Twitter chats, or engaging in Facebook communities related to the consultant's field enables direct interactions with potential clients and peers.

16. Competitor Analysis:

Understanding competitors' digital marketing strategies is insightful. It helps consultants adapt successful tactics while maintaining their unique brand identity.

17. Continuous Learning:

The digital marketing landscape evolves rapidly. Freelance consultants should commit to continuous learning, staying updated with the latest trends, tools, and best practices through online courses, webinars, and certifications.

The Digital Edge in Consulting Success

In today's digital age, a robust digital marketing and social media strategy is the edge that sets successful freelance consultants apart from the rest. It's the bridge that connects consultants to clients, expands their reach beyond borders, and establishes them as trusted experts in their fields. Whether they are optimizing their websites for SEO, crafting compelling content, or engaging with their audience on social media, every tactic plays a pivotal role in building a thriving freelance consulting career.

Digital marketing and social media tactics empower freelance consultants to tell their unique stories, share their knowledge, and connect with clients on a personal level. It's not merely about promoting services; it's about building relationships and establishing trust in a digital world where authenticity and expertise are prized.

In conclusion, the freelance consulting landscape has undergone a paradigm shift in recent years, driven by the digital revolution. Success in this field hinges on the ability to master the art of digital marketing and social media tactics. Freelance consultants who invest in these strategies and adapt to the evolving digital landscape are not only positioning themselves for success but are also contributing to the future of consulting in an increasingly interconnected world.

CHAPTER 3

Project Management

Navigating Client Expectations and Contracts: A Guide for New Freelance Consultants

For a freelance consultant just embarking on their journey, understanding and effectively managing client expectations while establishing robust contracts are critical elements of a successful consulting business. Freelancers are not just providers of services; they are partners in their clients' journeys to achieving their goals. In this guide, we'll explore the intricacies of managing client expectations and crafting contracts that foster strong, mutually beneficial client-consultant relationships.

1. Clear Communication is Key:

The foundation of successful client-consultant relationships is clear communication. From the initial consultation to project delivery, maintain open and honest lines of communication. Listen attentively to your clients' needs, ask clarifying questions, and ensure both parties are on the same page regarding project goals and deliverables.

2. Define Scope and Objectives:

Establish a well-defined project scope and objectives document. This document should outline the specific tasks, timelines, and deliverables for the project. Clarify what is included in your services and, equally important, what is not. This helps manage expectations from the outset.

3. Set Realistic Timelines:

Avoid overpromising and underdelivering. Provide realistic timelines for project completion, taking into account potential delays and unforeseen circumstances. Buffer your estimates to ensure you can meet or exceed expectations.

4. Transparent Pricing and Payment Terms:

Clearly outline your pricing structure and payment terms in your contract. Specify the payment schedule, methods, and any additional fees that may apply. Transparency in financial matters builds trust with clients.

5. Detailed Contracts:

Invest time in crafting detailed, legally binding contracts for each project. Contracts should include project scope, payment terms, deadlines, intellectual property rights, confidentiality clauses, dispute resolution processes, and any other relevant terms. If necessary, consult with a legal expert to ensure your contracts are comprehensive and enforceable.

6. Manage Scope Creep:

Scope creep occurs when a project's scope expands beyond its initial agreement. Be vigilant in monitoring and managing scope changes. If a client requests additional work, document it, discuss any impact on timelines and costs, and agree upon adjustments before proceeding.

7. Regular Updates and Progress Reports:

Keep clients informed about project progress. Regular updates and progress reports demonstrate your commitment to transparency and accountability. Share achievements, milestones, and any challenges encountered, along with proposed solutions.

8. Handle Challenges Professionally:

Challenges and obstacles are part of every project. When issues arise, address them professionally and promptly. Discuss potential solutions with your client and work collaboratively to overcome hurdles.

9. Manage Client Expectations Realistically:

While it's important to meet or exceed client expectations, it's equally crucial to set them realistically. Under-promising and over-delivering is a golden rule in consulting. If you believe a client's expectations are unattainable, diplomatically guide them toward more achievable goals.

10. Scope Change Requests:

When clients request changes to the project scope, assess the impact on timelines, costs, and resources. Document these changes in writing and obtain written approval from the client before proceeding. Adjust contracts and budgets accordingly.

11. Maintain Professional Boundaries:

While building rapport with clients is important, maintain professional boundaries. Avoid becoming overly familiar or emotionally involved in client relationships. Focus on delivering exceptional service and value.

12. Client Feedback and Reviews:

Encourage clients to provide feedback on your services. Constructive feedback helps you improve and strengthens the client-consultant relationship. Consider soliciting reviews or testimonials from satisfied clients to showcase your expertise to future prospects.

13. Underpromise and Overdeliver:

One of the best ways to exceed client expectations is to consistently underpromise and overdeliver. If you can complete a project ahead of schedule or offer additional value, it leaves a lasting positive impression.

14. Conflict Resolution:

Despite best efforts, conflicts may arise. Be prepared to handle them professionally and constructively. Have a dispute resolution process outlined in your contract to address disagreements, with mediation or arbitration as potential options.

15. Client Education:

Sometimes, clients may have unrealistic expectations due to a lack of understanding of the consulting process. Take the initiative to educate your clients about what to expect during the project, emphasizing the value you bring to the table.

16. Continuous Improvement:

After completing a project, conduct a post-mortem analysis. Reflect on what went well and what could be improved. Use this information to refine your processes and enhance your client relationships in future projects.

17. Documentation and Records:

Maintain detailed records of all project communications, including emails, agreements, and changes. Having a well-documented history can be invaluable in case of disputes or misunderstandings.

Effective management of client expectations and the creation of robust contracts are essential skills for freelance consultants starting their businesses. By fostering clear communication, setting realistic expectations, and providing exceptional service, freelance consultants can build strong, long-lasting client relationships that serve as the foundation of a successful consulting practice. Remember that successful consulting is not just about delivering services; it's about creating value, building trust, and helping clients achieve their objectives.

Project Planning, Execution, and Delivery for Newbie Freelance Consultants: A Roadmap to Success

For a freelance consultant just starting their journey, mastering the art of project planning, execution, and delivery is crucial. These skills form the backbone of a successful consulting career, enabling you to provide exceptional value to your clients, meet deadlines, and build a stellar reputation. In this guide, we'll walk through the key steps and strategies that every newbie freelance consultant should embrace to navigate these critical aspects of their business.

Project Planning: Laying the Foundation for Success

1. Client Needs Assessment:

Before you dive into project planning, ensure you have a thorough understanding of your client's needs and objectives. Conduct comprehensive interviews, surveys, or assessments to gather the necessary information.

2. Scope Definition:

Define the project scope clearly and concisely. What are the project's objectives, deliverables, and boundaries? Be meticulous in detailing what is included and what is not, to avoid scope creep later on.

3. Project Timeline:

Create a realistic project timeline. Break down the project into manageable phases or milestones, and allocate time for each. Consider potential bottlenecks or dependencies that may affect the schedule.

4. Resource Allocation:

Identify the resources required for the project, including personnel, tools, and materials. Ensure you have access to the necessary resources or make arrangements to acquire them.

5. Risk Assessment:

Identify potential risks that could impact the project. Develop a risk mitigation plan that outlines how you'll address these challenges if they arise.

6. Budget Planning:

Establish a budget that accounts for all project-related costs, including your fees, materials, software, and any subcontractors or experts you may need to hire.

7. Communication Strategy:

Define a clear communication strategy that outlines how you'll keep the client informed of project progress. Regular updates and milestones are key components of effective communication.

Project Execution: Bringing Your Plan to Life

1. Project Kickoff:

Begin the project with a kickoff meeting or session with your client. This is an opportunity to align expectations, introduce team members, and set the tone for collaboration.

2. Task Management:

Assign tasks to team members or yourself, if you're a solo consultant. Use project management tools and software to track progress, deadlines, and responsibilities.

3. Quality Assurance:
Maintain a focus on quality throughout the project. Review work regularly to ensure it aligns with the project's objectives and meets client expectations.

4. Client Collaboration:
Engage your client throughout the project. Seek their feedback, provide updates, and address any concerns promptly. Collaboration fosters transparency and client satisfaction.

5. Issue Resolution:
Challenges and roadblocks are inevitable in any project. Develop problem-solving skills and processes to address issues efficiently. Keep the client informed of any significant hurdles and your plans to overcome them.

6. Change Management:

If the project scope changes, document these changes and communicate them clearly to the client. Assess the impact on timelines, budgets, and resources and obtain client approval before proceeding.

Project Delivery: Exceeding Expectations

1. Final Quality Check:
Conduct a final quality check to ensure all project deliverables meet the agreed-upon standards and objectives.

2. Client Review and Feedback:
Share the project's final deliverables with the client for review. Encourage them to provide feedback and address any revisions or refinements needed.

3. Documentation and Reporting:
Provide the client with comprehensive documentation of the project, including a summary of work done, outcomes achieved, and any future recommendations. Report on how the project aligns with the initial objectives.

4. Client Handover:

If applicable, provide training or guidance to the client's team on how to use or maintain the project deliverables effectively.

5. Project Closure:

Conclude the project formally by acknowledging its completion. Thank the client for their collaboration and formally close out all project-related contracts and agreements.

6. Client Feedback and Testimonials:

Encourage clients to provide feedback on the project and your services. Positive testimonials and references can significantly enhance your reputation and attract future clients.

7. Evaluate and Learn:

After project delivery, take time to evaluate what went well and what could be improved. Use this feedback to refine your project management processes for future engagements.

Mastering project planning, execution, and delivery is essential for a newbie freelance consultant's success. These skills not only ensure you meet client expectations but also help you build lasting client relationships and a stellar professional reputation. By meticulously planning your projects, executing them with precision, and delivering exceptional results, you'll lay a strong foundation for a thriving consulting career.

Time Management and Productivity Tips for Newbie Freelance Consultant

Embarking on a freelance consulting career is an exciting venture, but it also demands impeccable time management and productivity skills. As a newbie in the consulting business, you'll soon discover that the ability to efficiently allocate your time and maximize productivity is essential for meeting deadlines, delivering exceptional value to clients, and maintaining a balanced work-life routine. In this guide, we'll explore time-tested time management and productivity tips to help you excel in your consulting journey.

1. Set Clear Goals and Priorities:

Begin each day or week by defining clear goals and priorities. Know what tasks need to be accomplished and in what order. This helps you stay focused on the most important and impactful activities.

2. Time Blocking:

Implement time blocking to allocate specific periods for different tasks or projects. This technique enhances concentration by minimizing multitasking and distractions.

3. Create a Schedule:

Develop a daily or weekly schedule that outlines your work hours and breaks. Stick to this schedule as closely as possible to establish a routine that optimizes your productivity.

4. Use Task Management Tools:

Leverage task management and project management tools like Trello, Asana, or Todoist to organize your tasks, set deadlines, and track progress. These tools streamline collaboration and keep you on track.

5. Prioritize High-Value Tasks:

Identify tasks that contribute the most to your project's success or client satisfaction. Prioritize these high-value tasks to ensure you're allocating your time wisely.

6. Eliminate Distractions:

Identify common distractions in your workspace and take measures to eliminate them. This may include silencing notifications, using website blockers, or designating a distraction-free workspace.

7. Set Realistic Deadlines:

Avoid overcommitting by setting realistic deadlines. Consider potential roadblocks and allocate buffer time for unexpected delays.

8. Time Tracking:

Use time tracking tools to monitor how you spend your work hours. This data can provide insights into where you can improve your efficiency.

9. Batch Similar Tasks:

Group similar tasks together and tackle them during designated time blocks. For instance, schedule email responses, research, or client meetings during specific windows to minimize context-switching.

10. Learn to Say No:

As a freelancer, you'll often receive requests for additional work or commitments. Be selective and learn to say no to projects or tasks that don't align with your goals or may overwhelm your schedule.

11. Delegate When Possible:

If you have the resources, consider delegating tasks that can be handled by others. This allows you to focus on high-priority activities that only you can complete.

12. Take Regular Breaks:

Don't underestimate the power of breaks. Short, frequent breaks can boost your productivity and creativity. Use techniques like the Pomodoro Technique (25 minutes of focused work followed by a 5-minute break) to maintain your productivity.

13. Stay Organized:

Keep your workspace and digital files organized. A clutter-free environment contributes to mental clarity and efficient work.

14. Continuous Learning:

Invest in continuous learning to enhance your skills and efficiency. Explore time management and productivity courses or books to discover new techniques and tools.

15. Limit Perfectionism:

Striving for excellence is admirable, but perfectionism can be a time drain. Learn when "good enough" is sufficient to move forward on a project.

16. Set Personal Boundaries:

Maintain a healthy work-life balance by setting personal boundaries. Clearly define when your workday ends and resist the temptation to overwork.

17. Reflect and Adjust:

Regularly evaluate your time management and productivity strategies. Identify areas where you can improve and make adjustments accordingly.

18. Seek Support and Feedback:

Connect with mentors or peers in the consulting field for guidance and feedback on your time management and productivity practices. They may offer valuable insights based on their experiences.

In conclusion, effective time management and productivity are essential skills for a newbie freelance consultant. By setting clear goals, managing your time wisely, eliminating distractions, and maintaining a healthy work-life balance, you'll not only excel in your consulting projects but also create a sustainable and fulfilling consulting career. Remember that productivity is a skill that can be developed and refined over time, so embrace these tips and continually strive for improvement in your consulting journey.

CHAPTER 4

Financial Management

Pricing Your Services and Crafting Winning Proposals: A Guide for Newbie Freelance Consultants

As a newbie freelance consultant, determining how to price your services and create compelling proposals is a critical step toward building a successful consulting business. Pricing reflects your value, while proposals are your first impression on potential clients. In this guide, we'll explore strategies for setting the right prices and crafting persuasive proposals that win projects and clients.

Pricing Your Services: Finding the Sweet Spot

1. Market Research:
   Start with market research to understand industry standards and competitive pricing. Explore what other consultants with similar expertise charge for their services. This will provide you with a benchmark.

2. Calculate Costs:

Calculate your overhead costs, including tools, software, workspace, insurance, and taxes. Ensure your pricing covers these expenses while allowing for a profit margin.

3. Determine Your Value:

Consider your qualifications, expertise, and the unique value you offer to clients. Your pricing should reflect the quality and results clients can expect from your services.

4. Hourly vs. Project-Based Pricing:

Decide whether you will charge clients hourly or offer project-based pricing. Project-based pricing provides transparency to clients and allows you to focus on delivering value rather than tracking hours.

5. Value-Based Pricing:

Consider value-based pricing, where you charge based on the perceived value of your services to the client. This approach can lead to higher fees when clients recognize the impact of your work on their business.

6. Tiered Pricing:

Offer tiered pricing options with varying levels of service or deliverables. This allows clients to choose a package that best suits their needs and budget.

7. Pricing Strategies:

Experiment with different pricing strategies such as retainer-based fees, performance-based bonuses, or subscription models to find what resonates with your target clients.

8. Flexibility and Negotiation:

Be open to negotiation, but maintain clear boundaries to avoid underpricing your services. Consider the specific needs and budget constraints of each client.

Creating Winning Proposals: Sealing the Deal

1. Understanding the Client:

Begin by thoroughly understanding the client's needs, challenges, and goals. Tailor your proposal to address their specific requirements.

2. Clear Project Scope:

Clearly define the scope of work in your proposal. Outline what you will deliver, the timeline, milestones, and any limitations or assumptions.

3. Highlight Your Expertise:

Showcase your expertise and qualifications. Explain why you are uniquely positioned to solve the client's problem or achieve their goals.

4. Client Benefits:

Emphasize the benefits the client will gain from your services. Address how your work will impact their business, whether it's increased revenue, cost savings, or improved efficiency.

5. Detailed Pricing:

Present your pricing clearly and transparently. Break down costs and fees to show the client what they are paying for. If you offer multiple pricing options, explain the differences between them.

6. Project Timeline:

Provide a timeline that outlines the project's key milestones and deadlines. This helps set client expectations and demonstrates your commitment to meeting deadlines.

7. Scope Changes:

Clearly define how scope changes will be handled and priced. Address the process for requesting and approving changes to avoid misunderstandings.

8. Terms and Conditions:

Include a section with terms and conditions, covering payment schedules, invoicing procedures, intellectual property rights, confidentiality, and dispute resolution processes.

9. Client Testimonials:

If possible, include client testimonials or references to build trust and demonstrate your track record of success.

10. Professional Formatting:

Present your proposal in a professional and organized format. Use clear headings, bullet points, and visuals to enhance readability.

11. Call to Action:

End your proposal with a compelling call to action, encouraging the client to take the next steps, whether it's signing the agreement, scheduling a call, or requesting further information.

12. Follow-Up:

After submitting your proposal, follow up with the client to answer any questions, address concerns, and gauge their interest. Timely follow-ups can significantly increase your chances of winning the project.

Continuous Improvement: Learning and Adapting

Remember that pricing and proposal creation are skills that can be refined over time. As you gain more experience in the consulting industry, continually assess your pricing strategy and proposal techniques. Seek feedback from satisfied clients and learned colleagues to identify areas for improvement.

By finding the right balance between pricing your services competitively and creating compelling proposals that demonstrate your expertise and value, you'll be well-equipped to attract clients and build a thriving freelance consulting business.

Budgeting, Invoicing, and Managing Cash Flow: Essential Financial Practices for Newbie Freelance Consultants

Financial management is a crucial aspect of a successful freelance consulting business. As a newbie in the consulting world, mastering budgeting, invoicing, and cash flow management is essential to ensure you maintain financial stability, meet your financial goals, and keep your business running smoothly. In this guide, we'll explore these financial practices to help you navigate your freelance consulting finances effectively.

1. Budgeting for Your Business:

Create a comprehensive budget that outlines your income, expenses, and financial goals. Consider the following steps:

- **Income Projections:** Estimate your expected income from consulting projects, factoring in your pricing strategy and expected project load.

- **Expense Tracking:** Keep meticulous records of your business expenses. Categorize expenses such as office supplies, software subscriptions, marketing costs, and any professional development investments.

  - Emergency Fund: Set aside a portion of your income as an emergency fund. This fund can provide a safety net for unexpected expenses or dry periods between projects.

  - Tax Planning: Budget for taxes by setting aside a percentage of your income for tax obligations. Consult with a tax professional to determine the appropriate tax withholding strategy for your situation.

  - Retirement Planning: Consider contributing to a retirement savings account, such as an Individual Retirement Account (IRA) or a Solo 401(k), to secure your financial future.

  - Business Growth: Allocate funds for business growth and marketing activities to attract new clients and expand your consulting practice.

2. Invoicing Best Practices:

Invoicing is a crucial part of your business operations. Ensure your invoicing process is efficient and effective:

- **Clear Invoices:** Create clear and professional invoices that include your business name, contact information, client details, payment terms, and a breakdown of services rendered with costs.

- **Timely Invoicing:** Send invoices promptly after completing a project or according to the agreed-upon schedule. Timely invoicing improves your cash flow.

- **Payment Terms:** Specify clear payment terms on your invoices, including due dates and accepted payment methods. Net-30 (payment within 30 days) is a common standard, but adapt this to your needs.

- **Late Payment Policies:** Communicate your policies regarding late payments and penalties for overdue invoices. Encourage prompt payment while maintaining professionalism.

- **Follow Up:** If clients do not remit payments on time, send polite but firm reminders. Maintain communication to resolve any issues and ensure timely payments.

- **Record Keeping:** Maintain organized records of all invoices, payments received, and outstanding balances. This helps you track your financial health and follow up on unpaid invoices.

3. Cash Flow Management:

Effective cash flow management is crucial to keep your business solvent and thriving:

- **Separate Business and Personal Finances:** Open a separate business bank account to manage your consulting income and expenses. This separation streamlines financial tracking and tax reporting.

- **Payment Schedules:** Coordinate your payment schedules with your client agreements. Ensure your expenses align with your cash flow, and set aside funds for taxes and savings regularly.

- **Payment Plans:** If possible, negotiate payment plans with clients for long-term projects to ensure a steady cash flow.

- **Emergency Fund:** Maintain a healthy emergency fund to cover unexpected expenses or periods with limited projects. Aim to save at least two to five months' worth of living expenses.

- **Cash Flow Forecasting:** Regularly assess your cash flow by projecting future income and expenses. This allows you to anticipate and address potential problems

- **Manage Debt Wisely:** Be cautious with taking on debt. If necessary, seek low-interest financing options and use debt strategically to invest in your business growth.

- **Consult a Financial Advisor:** If you're uncertain about managing your finances, consider consulting a financial advisor or accountant who specializes in freelance businesses. They can provide you with personalized guidance tailored to your unique situation.

By implementing strong budgeting practices, efficient invoicing procedures, and effective cash flow management, you'll be better equipped to navigate the financial aspects of your freelance consulting business. These practices not only ensure financial stability but also enable you to focus on delivering exceptional value to your clients and building a thriving consulting career.

Tax and Legal Considerations for Freelancer Newbies: Navigating the Business Landscape

As a newbie freelancer, understanding tax and legal considerations is essential for establishing a solid foundation for your business. While freelancing offers flexibility and independence, it also comes with responsibilities and obligations. In this guide, we'll explore the key tax and legal considerations that every freelancer should be aware of to ensure compliance and protect their business.

Tax Considerations:

1. Business Structure:
Decide on the legal structure for your business. Common options include sole proprietorship,

limited liability company (LLC), S corporation, and C corporation. Each has distinct tax implications, so choose the one that aligns with your goals.

2. Tax ID and Registration:

Depending on your location and business structure, you may need to obtain a federal Employer Identification Number (EIN) or a similar identification number for tax purposes. Register your business with the appropriate government authorities as needed.

3. Quarterly Estimated Taxes:

Freelancers are typically responsible for paying quarterly estimated taxes to cover income tax and self-employment tax. Failure to do so may result to problems. Calculate your estimated taxes accurately to avoid surprises at tax time.

4. Tax Deductions:

Keep thorough records of your business expenses. Many expenses related to your freelance work can be tax-deductible, such as home office expenses, equipment, software, and professional development.

5. Track Income and Expenses:

Use accounting software or spreadsheets to track your income and expenses throughout the year. This will simplify tax preparation and help you identify deductions.

6. Hire an Accountant:

Consider hiring a certified public accountant (CPA) or tax professional with experience working with freelancers. They can provide valuable guidance on tax planning and help you optimize your financial strategies.

7. Tax Deadlines:

Familiarize yourself with tax deadlines, including the filing deadline for your annual tax return and the due dates for quarterly estimated tax payments. Missing deadlines can result in having issues.

Legal Considerations:

1. Business Name and Registration:

If you choose to operate under a business name (other than your own), research the legal requirements for business name registration in your jurisdiction. This may involve registering a "doing business as" (DBA) name.

2. Contracts and Agreements:

Draft clear and comprehensive contracts for your clients. Contracts should outline project scope, payment terms, deadlines, confidentiality agreements, and other relevant terms. Consult with a legal professional if needed.

3. Business Licenses and Permits:

Determine whether your freelance business requires any specific licenses or permits based on your location and the services you provide. Failure to obtain necessary licenses can result in legal issues.

4. Insurance:

Evaluate the need for professional liability insurance, also known as errors and omissions (E&O) insurance. It can protect you from potential legal claims related to your consulting services.

5. Intellectual Property Rights:

Be clear about intellectual property rights, including who owns the work product, in your contracts. Address ownership, licensing, and usage rights to prevent disputes.

6. Client Data Protection:

If you handle client data, ensure compliance with data protection laws and maintain robust cybersecurity measures to protect sensitive information.

7. Taxes and Employment Law:

Comply with employment laws regarding freelancers and independent contractors in your area. Misclassification of workers can lead to legal consequences.

8. Non-Compete Agreements:

If you use non-compete agreements, ensure they are legally enforceable in your jurisdiction and reasonable in scope.

9. Legal Counsel:

Consult with an attorney experienced in freelance and small business law for personalized legal advice and guidance on legal matters.

Continual Learning and Compliance:

Freelancing offers incredible opportunities, but it also requires diligence in managing tax and legal aspects. Staying informed about tax law changes and consulting with legal and financial professionals when needed will help you navigate these complexities. By adhering to tax and legal best practices, you'll build a solid foundation for your freelance career and minimize the risk of legal issues down the road.

CHAPTER 5

Client Relations

Building and Maintaining Strong Client Relationships: A Guide for Freelance Consultant Newbies

As a newbie freelance consultant, your success doesn't solely depend on your expertise; it also hinges on your ability to build and maintain strong client relationships. Strong client relationships can lead to repeat business, referrals, and a thriving consulting career. In this guide, we'll explore key strategies to establish and nurture these valuable connections.

1. Understand Your Client's Needs:

Start by thoroughly understanding your client's goals, challenges, and expectations. Ask probing questions, actively listen, and seek to empathize with their perspective. The more you know about their needs, the better you can tailor your services to meet them.

2. Set Clear Expectations:

From the outset, establish clear and realistic expectations. Define the scope of work, project timeline, and deliverables. Transparency about what you will provide and what the client can expect fosters trust.

3. Effective Communication:

Maintain open and proactive communication with your clients. Respond to emails and messages promptly, provide regular updates on project progress, and be accessible when they have questions or concerns.

4. Be Reliable and Consistent:

Consistency is key to building trust.Deliver your work on time and as promised. Reliable performance builds your reputation as a consultant who can be counted on.

5. Exceed Expectations:

Strive to go above and beyond in your services. Surprise your clients by delivering results that exceed their initial expectations. These positive surprises leave a lasting impression.

6. Manage Expectations Realistically:

While exceeding expectations is important, it's equally crucial to manage them realistically. Avoid over-promising and under-delivering. Be transparent about what can and cannot be achieved.

7. Active Listening:

Actively listen to your clients' feedback and concerns. Show that you value their input and are willing to adapt and improve based on their insights.

8. Problem Solving:

Be solution-oriented when challenges arise. Instead of dwelling on problems, focus on finding effective solutions. Collaborate with your clients to address any issues that may arise during a project.

9. Consistent Quality:

Maintain consistent quality in your work. Strive to deliver excellence with every project. Consistency builds confidence in your abilities.

10. Personalized Service:

Tailor your services to each client's unique needs. Recognize that what works for one client may not work for another. Personalization demonstrates your commitment to their success.

11. Client Education:

Educate your clients about your processes, methodologies, and the value you bring to their projects. A well-informed client is more likely to appreciate your expertise.

12. Regular Check-Ins:

Schedule periodic check-in meetings with your clients, even when there are no immediate projects. These meetings can help you stay updated on their evolving needs and maintain a strong connection.

13. Celebrate Milestones:

Acknowledge project milestones and achievements. Celebrate successes, both big and small, with your clients. It builds a positive and collaborative atmosphere.

14. Seek Feedback:

Encourage clients to provide feedback on your services and performance. Constructive criticism can help you improve and strengthen your client relationships.

15. Gratitude and Appreciation:

Express your gratitude and appreciation for your clients' trust and business. A simple thank-you note or gesture can make clients feel valued.

16. Ask for Referrals:

If your clients are satisfied with your work, don't hesitate to ask for referrals. Satisfied clients are often willing to recommend you to their network.

17. Maintain Professional Boundaries:

While building rapport is important, maintain professional boundaries. Avoid becoming overly familiar or sharing personal information that is not relevant to the project.

18. Address Conflicts Gracefully:

Conflicts can occur in any business relationship. Address them professionally, calmly, and constructively. Focus on finding mutually beneficial solutions.

19. Follow Up After Project Completion:

After a project concludes, follow up with your clients to ensure they are satisfied and inquire if they need any further assistance. It demonstrates your commitment to their long-term success.

20. Continuous Improvement:

Continually assess your client relationships and seek ways to enhance them. Adapt your approach based on feedback and evolving client needs.

By implementing these strategies, you'll be well on your way to establishing strong client relationships as a freelance consultant. Building trust, delivering value, and maintaining effective communication will not only help you succeed in your consulting career but also lead to lasting client partnerships and business growth.

Handling Difficult Clients and Conflicts: A Freelance Consultant's Guide

Dealing with difficult clients and conflicts is an inevitable part of freelance consulting. While most clients are pleasant to work with, there may be instances where challenges arise. As a freelance consultant, it's essential to have strategies in place to address difficult situations professionally and effectively. Here's a guide to help you navigate these challenges:

1. Stay Calm and Professional:

Maintaining composure is paramount when dealing with difficult clients or conflicts. Respond to their concerns or frustrations with a calm and professional demeanor. Avoid becoming defensive or emotional.

2. Active Listening:

Listen actively to your client's concerns. Allow them to express their feelings and frustrations. Sometimes, clients simply want to be heard, and listening attentively can diffuse tension.

3. Empathize and Show Understanding:

Express empathy and understanding for your client's perspective. Acknowledge their feelings and reassure them that you are committed to finding a resolution.

4. Clarify Expectations:

If the conflict arises from miscommunication or differing expectations, take the opportunity to clarify the project scope, deliverables, and timelines. Ensure both parties have a shared understanding.

5. Focus on Solutions:

Shift the conversation toward finding solutions. Propose actionable steps to address the client's concerns and improve the situation. Collaborate on a plan to move forward.

6. Set Boundaries:

If a client's behavior becomes disrespectful or crosses boundaries, politely but firmly establish your professional boundaries. Respect should be mutual in any working relationship.

7. Document Everything:

Keep a detailed record of all interactions, emails, messages, and agreements related to the project and the conflict. These records can be valuable if the situation escalates or if you need to refer back to previous discussions.

8. Seek a Third Party:

If communication breaks down, consider involving a neutral third party, such as a mediator or an industry association, to help facilitate a resolution. Mediation can often bridge gaps in communication.

9. Contractual Agreements:

Review your contract and any terms and conditions that were agreed upon at the start of the project. Ensure that you are both adhering to the contractual obligations.

10. Escalate as a Last Resort:

Escalation should be a last resort. If all attempts to resolve the conflict fail, consider involving a legal advisor or seeking legal remedies, but only after carefully evaluating the situation and seeking professional advice.

11. Learn and Prevent:

After resolving a conflict, take time to reflect on the experience. Analyze what went wrong and how similar issues can be prevented in the future. Use the conflict as a learning opportunity for personal and professional growth.

12. Set Clear Expectations for Future Work:

If you decide to continue working with a client after a conflict, establish clear expectations for future projects. Address any concerns or misunderstandings proactively to prevent further conflicts.

13. Trust Your Intuition:

Sometimes, it may be in your best interest to part ways with a difficult client if the working relationship is consistently unproductive or harmful. Trust your intuitions and prioritize your well-being.

Remember that conflicts are a natural part of business, and how you handle them can define your professionalism and reputation. While it's essential to address issues promptly and professionally, your ultimate goal should be to find resolutions that benefit both parties and preserve a positive working relationship whenever possible.

CHAPTER 6

Professional Growth

Continuous Learning and Skill Improvement: The Cornerstones of Success for Newbie Freelance Consultants

In the dynamic world of freelance consulting, staying ahead of the curve is not only beneficial but essential for success. Continuous learning and skill improvement are the cornerstones of a thriving freelance consulting career. As a newbie in the industry, here's why and how you should make lifelong learning a priority:

1. Adapt to Market Changes:
    Industries evolve, technologies advance, and client needs change. Staying up-to-date with market trends and industry developments is crucial to adapt your services and remain relevant.

2. Enhance Expertise:
    Continuous learning allows you to deepen your expertise in your chosen field. The more

knowledgeable you are, the more value you can offer to clients, which can lead to higher demand for your services.

3. Diversify Your Skill Set:

Expanding your skill set beyond your core expertise can open up new opportunities. For example, a digital marketing consultant may benefit from learning about data analytics or graphic design.

4. Build Confidence:

Confidence in your abilities is a key factor in attracting and retaining clients. Continuous learning boosts your confidence as you acquire new knowledge and skills.

5. Competitive Advantage:

In a competitive freelance market, continuous learning sets you apart from others. It shows potential clients that you are committed to providing the best possible solutions.

6. Problem Solving:

Learning equips you with problem-solving skills to tackle complex client challenges effectively. You can offer innovative solutions based on your updated knowledge.

7. Networking Opportunities:

Engaging in learning activities, such as workshops, seminars, or online courses, provides opportunities to network with peers, industry experts, and potential clients.

8. Embrace Technology:

Technology plays a significant role in freelance consulting. Regularly updating your tech skills ensures you can leverage the latest tools and platforms to deliver results.

9. Stay Informed About Regulations:

Depending on your field, regulations and compliance requirements may change. Continuous learning helps you stay informed about legal and regulatory updates that affect your work.

10. Invest in Personal Growth:

Learning isn't limited to professional skills. Personal development, such as communication, time management, and negotiation skills, also contributes to your success as a freelance consultant.

How to Embrace Continuous Learning:

1. Set Learning Goals:

Define your learning objectives. What skills or knowledge areas do you want to improve? Setting clear goals enables you to be focused and motivated.

2. Allocate Time for Learning:

Dedicate a portion of your schedule to learning activities. This might include reading industry publications, taking online courses, attending webinars, or joining professional organizations.

3. Learn from Experience:

Reflect on your consulting projects and extract lessons learned. Analyze what went well and what could be improved, and apply these insights to future work.

4. Seek Feedback:

Request feedback from clients and colleagues. Their input can help you identify areas for improvement and tailor your learning efforts accordingly.

5. Build a Learning Network:

Connect with mentors, industry experts, and fellow freelancers who can provide guidance and share knowledge.

6. Utilize Online Resources:

The internet is a treasure trove of learning resources. Explore online courses, webinars, forums, and blogs related to your field.

7. Invest in Self-Paced Learning:

Self-paced courses and tutorials allow you to learn at your own speed and convenience. Platforms like Coursera, LinkedIn Learning, and Udemy offer a wide range of options.

8. Attend Workshops and Conferences:

Whenever possible, attend industry-specific workshops, conferences, and seminars. These events provide valuable insights and networking opportunities.

9. Document Your Learning:

Keep a learning journal to record new skills, knowledge, and experiences. Review your progress regularly to see how far you've come.

10. Embrace a Growth Mindset:

Emphasize a growth mindset, which means viewing challenges as opportunities for learning and improvement. Embrace setbacks and learn from them.

Remember that continuous learning is not a one-time endeavor but a lifelong commitment. The freelance consulting landscape is ever-changing, and those who embrace learning and skill improvement are better equipped to thrive in this dynamic industry. By investing in your own growth and development, you're not only benefiting your career but also providing greater value to your clients.

Staying Up-to-Date in the Consulting Business: A Guide for Newbie Freelance Consultants

The consulting industry is marked by constant change and innovation. To succeed as a freelance consultant, it's imperative to stay up-to-date with industry trends, emerging technologies, and evolving client needs. Here's a comprehensive guide on how newbie freelance consultants can keep their knowledge and skills current:

1. Set Learning Goals:

Begin by setting specific learning goals. Determine what aspects of your field or niche you want to stay updated on. These goals will guide your learning journey.

2. Follow Industry Publications:

Subscribe to industry-specific magazines, journals, newsletters, and blogs. These publications often feature the latest trends, case studies, and expert insights.

3. Join Professional Associations:

Consider becoming a member of professional associations related to your consulting niche. These organizations often offer access to resources, webinars, conferences, and networking opportunities.

4. Attend Workshops and Conferences:

Whenever possible, attend workshops, conferences, and seminars in your industry. These events provide a wealth of knowledge and opportunities to network with peers and experts.

5. Online Learning Platforms:

Enroll in online courses and platforms like Coursera, LinkedIn Learning, edX, or Udemy. These platforms offer a wide range of courses, including those focused on the latest industry trends.

6. Webinars and Podcasts:

Participate in webinars and listen to podcasts related to your field. Many experts share their insights and experiences through these channels.

7. Join Online Forums and Communities:

Become a member of online forums and communities dedicated to your niche. Engaging in discussions with peers can help you stay informed about current industry challenges and solutions.

8. Network with Peers and Mentors:

Build a professional network by connecting with peers, mentors, and experienced consultants in your field. They can provide valuable guidance and share their experiences.

9. Follow Thought Leaders:

Identify thought leaders and influencers in your industry and follow them on social media platforms like LinkedIn and Twitter. They often share valuable insights and articles.

10. Diversify Your Learning Sources:

Don't rely on a single source for information. Diversify your learning sources to gain a well-rounded perspective on industry trends and developments.

11. Experiment and Innovate:

Be open to experimenting with new ideas, tools, and techniques in your consulting practice. Innovation often stems from trying new approaches.

12. Client Feedback:

Pay close attention to client feedback. Clients may provide insights into the changing landscape of their industry or emerging challenges they face.

13. Monitor Competitors:

Keep an eye on your competitors. Analyze their strategies and offerings to understand how they adapt to industry changes.

14. Continual Self-Assessment:

Regularly assess your own skills and knowledge gaps. Identify areas where you need improvement and prioritize learning in those domains.

15. Time Management:

Allocate dedicated time for learning in your weekly or monthly schedule. Treat it as an essential part of your business.

16. Stay Tech-Savvy:

Given the digital nature of consulting, stay updated on relevant technologies and software tools that can enhance your services.

17. Adaptation and Flexibility:

Be willing to adapt and pivot your consulting approach based on new insights and trends. Flexibility is a valuable trait in a changing industry.

Remember that staying up-to-date in the consulting business is not a one-time effort but a continuous commitment to lifelong learning. By actively pursuing knowledge and remaining adaptable to change, newbie freelance consultants can build thriving consulting careers that provide value to clients in an ever-evolving business landscape.

Building Portfolios and Testimonials: A Strategy Guide for Newbie Freelance Consultants

For newbie freelance consultants, establishing a strong portfolio and collecting client testimonials are essential steps to showcase your expertise, credibility, and trustworthiness in the competitive consulting industry. Here's a comprehensive strategy guide on how to effectively build your portfolio and gather valuable testimonials:

1. Start with Pro Bono Work:

As a newbie, consider offering your consulting services for free or at a reduced rate to a select few clients. This allows you to gain real-world experience, build your portfolio, and gather initial testimonials.

2. Select Niche Projects:

Choose projects that align with your expertise and passion, even if they're unpaid initially. Focusing on your niche will help you build a specialized portfolio.

3. Create Case Studies:

After completing projects, write detailed case studies that showcase the challenges, solutions, and results achieved for your clients. Include before-and-after statistics, if applicable.

4. Build a Professional Website:

Invest in a professional website to host your portfolio. Create a dedicated section for case studies, testimonials, and client success stories.

5. Visual Appeal:

Ensure your portfolio is visually appealing and easy to navigate. Use high-quality images, infographics, and graphics to illustrate your work.

6. Content Quality:

Craft well-written, compelling descriptions for each portfolio item. Highlight your role, the problem you solved, and the impact of your solution on the client's business.

7. Ask for Permission:

Always seek your clients' permission before featuring their projects in your portfolio. Some clients may have confidentiality concerns.

8. Collect Testimonials:

Reach out to satisfied clients and request testimonials. Encourage them to provide specific details about the value you brought to their project and their overall experience working with you.

9. Video Testimonials:

Video testimonials can be particularly convincing. If clients are willing, record short video testimonials highlighting their positive experiences.

10. LinkedIn Recommendations:

Request recommendations on LinkedIn from clients and colleagues who can vouch for your consulting skills and professionalism.

11. Refresh Your Portfolio Regularly:

Keep your portfolio up-to-date with your latest projects and achievements. Potential clients want to see your recent work.

12. Variety Matters:

Aim to diversify your portfolio by showcasing projects from different industries or aspects of your consulting services. This demonstrates versatility.

13. Tell a Story:

Use storytelling techniques in your case studies and testimonials. Describe the client's initial challenges, the journey to a solution, and the positive outcomes.

14. Highlight Client Feedback:

Include excerpts from client emails or messages that express satisfaction with your work. These informal comments can carry weight.

15. Local Business Partnerships:

Partner with local businesses or startups and offer your consulting services at a reduced rate in exchange for the opportunity to include them in your portfolio.

16. Continuously Improve:

As you gain more experience and gather testimonials, continually improve your portfolio presentation and content to reflect your growth as a consultant.

17. Ethical Considerations:

Maintain ethical standards when building your portfolio and gathering testimonials. Never fabricate results or testimonials, as this can damage your reputation.

18. Seek Feedback on Your Portfolio:

Ask trusted colleagues or mentors for feedback on your portfolio. They can provide valuable suggestions for improvement.

Building a compelling portfolio and collecting authentic testimonials is an ongoing process. As you gain experience and successfully complete more projects, your portfolio and testimonials will become powerful tools to attract new clients, establish trust, and demonstrate your expertise as a newbie freelance consultant.

CHAPTER 7

Balancing Work and Life

Avoiding Burnout and Managing Stress: Essential Tips for Newbie Freelance Consultants

The freelance consulting journey can be incredibly rewarding, but it also comes with its fair share of challenges that can lead to burnout and stress. As a newbie freelance consultant, it's crucial to prioritize your well-being and adopt strategies to manage stress effectively. Here are essential tips to help you avoid burnout and maintain a healthy work-life balance:

1. Set Realistic Work Hours:

Establish clear boundaries for your work hours. Define when your workday starts and ends, and stick to these limits as closely as possible. Avoid overworking to maintain work-life balance.

2. Create a Dedicated Workspace:

Designate a specific area in your home as your workspace. This separation helps you mentally switch between work and personal life.

3. Plan Your Schedule:
Organize your work tasks and schedule them in advance. Prioritize important tasks and allocate specific time slots for focused work.

4. Take Regular Breaks:
Incorporate short breaks throughout your workday. Use this time to stretch, walk, or do relaxation exercises to recharge your mind.

5. Exercise and Stay Active:
Regular physical activity is an excellent stress reliever. Find an exercise routine that you enjoy and make it a part of your daily or weekly schedule.

6. Practice Mindfulness and Meditation:
Mindfulness techniques and meditation can help reduce stress and improve focus. Dedicate time each day for mindfulness exercises.

7. Limit Multitasking:

Avoid the temptation to juggle multiple tasks simultaneously. Focus on one task at a time to improve productivity and reduce stress.

8. Set Realistic Goals:

Establish achievable goals for your consulting projects. Unrealistic expectations can lead to frustration and burnout.

9. Learn to Say No:

As a newbie, you might be inclined to take on every project. However, it's essential to recognize your limitations and decline projects that may overwhelm you.

10. Delegate When Possible:

If you have the opportunity, delegate tasks that are outside your expertise or that can be handled by others. This frees up your time for critical responsibilities.

11. Seek Social Support:

Stay connected with friends and family. Share your challenges and concerns with a support system that understands and can provide emotional support.

12. Limit Distractions:

Identify common distractions and take steps to minimize them. Turn off non-essential notifications, and consider using website blockers during work hours.

13. Time Management Tools:

Utilize time management apps and tools to track your tasks and stay organized. Tools like Trello, Asana, or Notion can help you manage projects efficiently.

14. Prioritize Self-Care:

Dedicate time to self-care activities you enjoy, whether it's reading, hobbies, or spending time with loved ones. Taking care of yourself is essential for long-term well-being.

15. Get Adequate Sleep:

Ensure you get enough quality sleep. Poor sleep can exacerbate stress and negatively impact your performance.

16. Seek Professional Help:

If you find yourself struggling with chronic stress or burnout symptoms, don't hesitate to seek support from a mental health professional or counselor.

17. Celebrate Achievements:

Acknowledge and celebrate your achievements, no matter how small. Positive reinforcement can boost your motivation and reduce stress.

18. Set Boundaries with Clients:

Communicate clear boundaries with clients regarding response times and availability. Ensure they understand when you are available for work-related inquiries.

19. Take Time Off:

Schedule regular breaks and vacations. Disconnect from work completely during your time off to recharge.

20. Continuous Learning:

Invest in your professional development and continuously improve your consulting skills. Feeling competent in your role can reduce stress.

Remember that avoiding burnout and managing stress is an ongoing process. It's essential to regularly assess your work habits, make adjustments, and prioritize self-care to maintain your physical and mental well-being as a newbie freelance consultant. By taking proactive steps, you can ensure a more fulfilling and sustainable consulting career.

Setting Boundaries and Maintaining Work-Life Balance:

As a newbie freelance consultant, establishing clear boundaries and maintaining a healthy work-life balance is essential for your well-being and long-term success. Freelancing offers flexibility, but it can also blur the lines between work and personal life. Here's a comprehensive guide on how to set boundaries and achieve balance in your freelance consulting career:

1. Define Your Work Hours:
Establish specific work hours that align with your productivity and personal preferences. Communicate these hours to your clients, colleagues, and yourself

2. Set Clear Expectations:

Communicate your availability, response times, and turnaround expectations to clients upfront. Be realistic about what you can deliver within your defined work hours.

3. Limit Availability:

Resist the urge to be constantly available to clients or respond to work-related messages during non-work hours. Set boundaries for email and communication outside of your defined work time.

4. Prioritize Self-Care:

Schedule regular self-care activities such as exercise, hobbies, and spending time with loved ones. Treat these commitments with the same importance as client meetings.

5. Take Breaks:

Incorporate short breaks into your workday to recharge. These breaks can help prevent burnout and improve overall productivity.

6. Learn to Say No:

Be selective when accepting new projects. Overcommitting can lead to excessive stress and compromise your work-life balance.

7. Delegate When Possible:

If you have the resources, consider delegating tasks or outsourcing aspects of your work to allow you more time for personal life and relaxation.

8. Set Boundaries with Technology:

Turn off work-related notifications and devices during your non-work hours. Create a physical separation between your work and personal devices if possible.

9. Establish Buffer Times:

Schedule buffer times between meetings or client work to accommodate unforeseen delays or to allow yourself brief moments of rest.

10. Utilize Time Management Tools:

Use time management apps or tools to manage your tasks and stay organized. These tools can help you work efficiently and reduce work-related stress.

11. Set Long-Term Goals:

Define your long-term career goals and personal aspirations. Having a clear vision can guide your decision-making and prevent you from getting lost in the daily grind.

12. Learn to Disconnect:

After completing your work for the day, mentally disconnect from work-related thoughts and stressors. Engage in relaxing activities to transition into your personal life.

13. Batch Tasks:

Group similar tasks together and batch them for efficient completion. This approach can free up more time for other aspects of your life.

14. Manage Client Expectations:

Communicate your boundaries and work processes to clients at the beginning of your collaboration. Be transparent about what they can expect in terms of communication and availability.

15. Seek Support:

Share your boundary-setting goals with friends, family, or fellow freelancers who can hold you accountable and offer support.

16. Review and Adjust:

Periodically assess how well you are maintaining your work-life balance. Adjust your boundaries and strategies as needed to ensure you stay on track.

17. Financial Planning:

Establish a clear financial plan and budget to ensure you can support your desired work-life balance without unnecessary financial stress.

18. Practice Self-Reflection:

Regularly reflect on your work-life balance and its impact on your well-being. Adjust your approach based on your evolving needs and priorities.

19. Celebrate Achievements:

Acknowledge and celebrate your successes in maintaining a healthy work-life balance. Recognize that balance is an ongoing achievement.

Maintaining work-life balance as a newbie freelance consultant requires conscious effort and discipline. By setting boundaries, communicating effectively with clients, and prioritizing self-care, you can create a work environment that supports both your professional and personal goals. Achieving balance will not only improve your overall well-being but also enhance your productivity and longevity in the freelance consulting world.

CHAPTER 8

Exploring Potential Avenues for Growth and Expansion as a Freelance Consultant

As a freelance consultant, your journey doesn't have to be confined to a single niche or limited scope of services. To achieve sustained growth and expansion, it's essential to explore various avenues that can broaden your consulting horizons. Here's a comprehensive guide on how to identify and pursue potential avenues for growth and expansion in your freelance consulting career:

1. Diversify Your Service Offerings:
Consider expanding your range of consulting services to address a broader spectrum of client needs. If you specialize in one area, explore related services or complementary expertise.

2. Explore New Industries or Niches:
Investigate industries or niches where your skills can be applied effectively. Entering new markets can open doors to fresh opportunities.

3. Collaborate with Other Consultants:

Partner with fellow consultants who possess complementary skills. Collaborations can lead to joint ventures, cross-referrals, and access to a wider client base.

4. International Expansion:

Leverage technology to offer your consulting services to clients in different regions or countries. Understand the specific needs and regulations of international markets.

5. Online Courses and Workshops:

Share your expertise through online courses, webinars, and workshops. This can establish you as a thought leader in your field and generate additional income.

6. Publish Books or Ebooks:

Write and publish books or ebooks on topics related to your consulting niche. This not only enhances your credibility but also creates a passive income stream.

7. Speaking Engagements:

Offer keynote speeches or workshops at industry conferences and events. Public speaking can help you reach a larger audience and attract potential clients.

8. Create Digital Products:

Develop digital products like templates, toolkits, or software solutions that can be sold to clients seeking DIY solutions.

9. Subscription-Based Services:

Consider offering subscription-based consulting services, where clients pay a recurring fee for ongoing access to your expertise.

10. Niche Marketing:

Specialize in a specific niche within your consulting field. Becoming a niche expert can make you highly sought after by clients seeking specialized solutions.

11. White Label Services:

Offer your consulting services as a white-label solution to other businesses, agencies, or consultants. They can resell your services under their brand.

12. Mentorship and Coaching:

Share your knowledge and experience by becoming a mentor or coach for aspiring consultants. This can be a fulfilling way to give back and generate income.

13. Strategic Alliances:

Form strategic alliances with businesses or organizations that can refer clients to you or provide opportunities for collaboration.

14. Continuous Learning:

Invest in your professional development by staying up-to-date with industry trends and acquiring new skills that align with potential growth areas.

15. Market Research:

Conduct thorough market research to identify emerging needs and gaps in the consulting landscape. Tailor your services to address these gaps.

16. Networking:

Attend industry events, join professional associations, and engage in networking to connect with potential clients, partners, and collaborators.

17. Client Feedback:

Listen to your clients' feedback and needs. Adapt and evolve your services based on their input to better serve them and attract new clients.

18. Invest in Marketing and Branding:

Enhance your online presence and branding to increase visibility and attract a broader client base.

19. Scalable Systems:

Develop scalable systems and processes that can handle increased demand efficiently as your consulting practice grows.

20. Strategic Planning:

Create a strategic growth plan that outlines your goals, target markets, marketing strategies, and expansion initiatives. Regularly review and adjust your plan as needed.

Remember that growth and expansion in your freelance consulting career may involve taking calculated risks and stepping outside your comfort zone. Stay adaptable, open to change, and willing to embrace new challenges. By exploring these potential avenues, you can not only expand your client base but also build a fulfilling and thriving consulting practice.